Franklin School
Summit Public Schools

ALL ABOUT
PULLEYS

James De Medeiros

LIGHTBOX
openlightbox.com

Go to
www.openlightbox.com
and enter this book's unique code.

ACCESS CODE

LBL87754

Lightbox is an all-inclusive digital solution for the teaching and learning of curriculum topics in an original, groundbreaking way. Lightbox is based on National Curriculum Standards.

STANDARD FEATURES OF LIGHTBOX

AUDIO High-quality narration using text-to-speech system

ACTIVITIES Printable PDFs that can be emailed and graded

SLIDESHOWS Pictorial overviews of key concepts

VIDEOS Embedded high-definition video clips

WEBLINKS Curated links to external, child-safe resources

TRANSPARENCIES Step-by-step layering of maps, diagrams, charts, and timelines

INTERACTIVE MAPS Interactive maps and aerial satellite imagery

QUIZZES Ten multiple choice questions that are automatically graded and emailed for teacher assessment

KEY WORDS Matching key concepts to their definitions

Copyright © 2017 Smartbook Media Inc. All rights reserved.

Simple Machines

CONTENTS

Lightbox Access Code.................. 2

The Pulley.. 4

Simple Machines 6

Using Pulleys 8

Pulleys of the World 10

Ancient Pulleys 12

Pulleys Timeline 13

Force and Movement................ 14

Working with Force..................... 16

How Pulleys Work....................... 18

What Is a
Manufacturing Engineer?......... 20

Brain Teasers 21

Pulleys in Action 22

Key Words/Index......................... 23

Log on to
www.openlightbox.com............ 24

All About Pulleys

The Pulley

A pulley is a wheel that spins easily on its **axle**. A groove on the outside edge of the wheel helps hold a rope or **cable** in place around the wheel. Pulling on one side of the rope causes the rope to slide through the pulley. This can move a load attached to the other end of the rope. Elevators, farming tools, and many types of aircraft all have pulleys.

The pulley is a type of simple machine. A machine is a device that uses power to do a task. There are six kinds of simple machines. They are the inclined plane, the lever, the pulley, the screw, the wedge, and the wheel and axle. All simple machines make **work** easier. However, they do not add any **energy** of their own to help people do work. Instead, simple machines change the **effort** needed to perform tasks.

 In the 1400s, Leonardo da Vinci drew **more than 500** sketches of flying machines, many of which had pulleys.

The world's **first passenger elevator**, run by an electric motor and pulleys, was used in 1857.

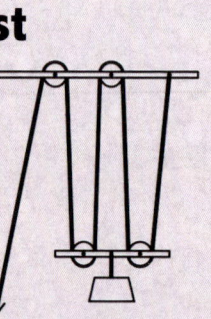 **More than 400** farm pulleys are on display at the Lewis and Clark Pulley Museum in Nebraska.

4 Simple Machines

Rock climbing relies on the use of pulleys.

All About Pulleys 5

Simple Machines

The inclined plane and the lever are the most basic of all simple machines. They can even be found in other types of simple machines.

Types of Inclined Planes

The **inclined plane** is the **simplest** of the simple machines. Any **slope**, such as a hill, is an inclined plane.

A **wedge** is two inclined planes put **together**.

A **screw** is an inclined plane **wrapped** around a center bar.

Types of Levers

A **lever** is a bar that rests on a **pivot or fulcrum**. Pushing down on one end of the bar helps to **lift** a load on the other end of the bar.

A **wheel and axle** is a lever in which the bar **circles** around the fulcrum, or axle.

A **pulley** is a lever that uses a **wheel** for the fulcrum and a **rope** instead of a bar.

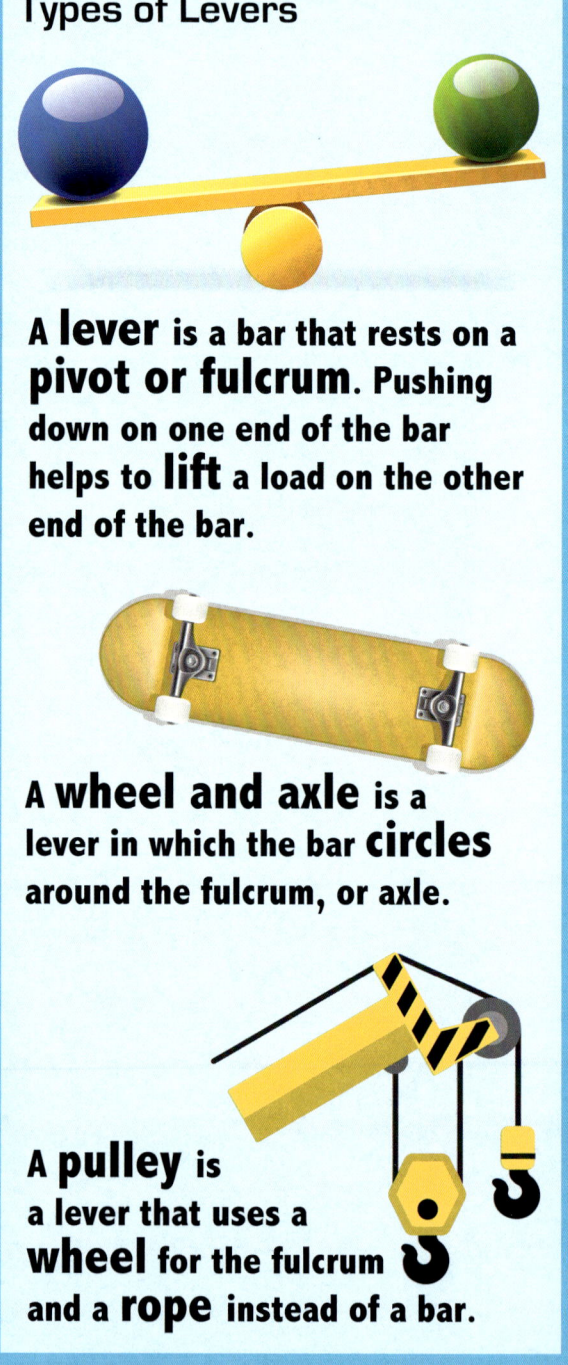

Simple Machines

From Simple to Complex

Simple machines can be combined to make other kinds of machines. When simple machines are combined, the new device is often called a compound or complex machine. Pulleys work together with other simple machines to create many devices used today.

Airplane
An airplane uses pulleys to move the **rudder** on its tail. The plane's wings are wedges. Wheels and axles help the plane take off and land.

Bicycle
A bicycle has pulleys that change which **gear** is used to move the vehicle. The pulleys are attached to a lever. Gears are a type of wheel and axle. Screws help hold parts of the bicycle together.

Crane
A crane uses levers and pulleys to move heavy loads. Levers help control the movement of the crane. Pulleys are used to lift the load into place.

All About Pulleys

Using Pulleys

Pulleys most often use rope to lift a load. However, the rope must be strong enough to support the load's weight. Very heavy loads may require a pulley with a steel cable, which is stronger than rope. A winch, or drum with cables wound around it, uses many pulleys at once to lift heavy loads. Winches are used at building construction sites and in factories where large, heavy machines are made.

Some pulleys operate with a belt instead of a rope or cable. This type of pulley is called a belt drive or drive belt. When a wheel turns, the belt wrapped around it turns as well. This transfers power from that wheel to other wheels connected to the belt. Automobile engines and many types of electric motors use belt drives.

A bicycle chain is a type of belt drive.

Pulleys at Work

People use pulleys every day to make their work easier. There are three types of pulleys. They are the fixed pulley, the movable pulley, and the compound pulley. Each type operates in a different way.

Helicopter Pulleys
A pulley attached to a helicopter is an example of a fixed pulley. A fixed pulley is held in place at a single spot. This pulley is useful when pulling down on a rope is easier than lifting a load. Helicopters use fixed pulleys for tasks such as collecting water from oceans or lakes to put out fires on land.

Construction Cranes
The pulleys on a construction crane are examples of movable pulleys. This kind of pulley moves with the load. The effort applied by the user on the pulley is increased, requiring less effort to lift the load.

Sailboats
The pulleys on a sailboat are examples of compound pulleys. A compound pulley uses a combination of fixed and movable pulleys. Rope is threaded between the pulleys. Sailboats use compound pulleys to lift and lower sails.

All About Pulleys

Pulleys of the World

People around the world use pulleys in their daily lives. Clotheslines, curtains, window blinds, and other household items have pulleys. Large pieces of equipment used in transportation rely on pulleys as well.

2 FRANCE A pulley is used on a zip line, which carries people in mid-air from one end of a cable to another. The world's highest zip line runs between the Orelle and Val Thorens ski resorts at a height of 10,597 feet (3,230 meters).

1 UNITED STATES Scientists working near Kaktovik, Alaska, use pulleys to weigh polar bears. The bears are weighed to check their health.

NORTH AMERICA

ATLANTIC OCEAN

PACIFIC OCEAN

SOUTH AMERICA

0   2,000 Kilometers
0   1,000 Miles

Simple Machines

Pulleys are helpful to scientists. They are also used by people taking part in a variety of sports. This map shows places around the world where pulleys are in use today.

3

BELGIUM Pulleys are used to transport boats between rivers of different heights. The top of the Strépy-Thieu boat lift in the Canal du Centre is 384 feet (117 m) high, making it the tallest lift of its kind.

4

NEPAL AND CHINA With an elevation of 29,035 feet (8,850 m), Mount Everest is the highest point on Earth. Pulleys are part of the gear used by climbers for going up and down the mountain.

All About Pulleys 11

Ancient Pulleys

Pulleys have been used for thousands of years. In Mesopotamia, a region in the ancient Middle East, pulleys may have been used to lift jars of water as early as 1500 BC. The ancient Greek scientist Archimedes invented the compound pulley in about 250 BC. Throughout history, people have used pulleys to build many tall structures. Those structures include Notre Dame Cathedral in Paris, France.

For centuries, pulleys have been important tools on sailing ships. When pulleys are used to raise or lower a sail, the amount of wind hitting the ship's sails increases or decreases. Sailors use this difference to change the speed of the ship.

Almost 2,000 years ago, pulleys and other simple machines were used to build the Colosseum, a large stadium in Rome, Italy.

Simple Machines

Pulleys Timeline

About 250 BC
Archimedes pulls a boat onto land with a compound pulley.

About 500 BC
The Greeks use pulleys in theaters to lower actors to the stage.

AD 70
Construction on the Colosseum begins.

1345
Notre Dame Cathedral in Paris is completed.

1913
Henry Ford builds a **conveyor belt** that uses pulleys, which speeds up production of cars at his factory in Michigan.

1916
In Tennessee, Ernest Holmes invents the tow truck, which uses pulleys to lift cars.

1960s
The world's longest conveyor belt is built. It runs almost 61 miles (98 kilometers) from a mine in Africa's Sahara Desert to the Atlantic Ocean.

2003
The *Mirabella V*, the world's largest single-mast yacht, is built. The boat has pulleys to adjust its sails.

2005
Kingda Ka, the world's tallest roller coaster, is built in New Jersey. It uses a pulley to pull the cars up 456 feet (139 m).

All About Pulleys 13

Rockets must use a great deal of force to reach outer space.

Force and Movement

Force is a push or a pull that causes an object to move or change its direction. When an object is not moving, or is at rest, all of the forces pushing or pulling on it are in balance. This balance is called equilibrium.

When scientists study forces and how objects move, there are three measurements they take into account. They figure out an object's weight, how fast it is moving, and the amount of force that is causing the object to move. Understanding forces, how forces affect objects, and how objects affect each other can make it easier to move objects.

Friction and Gravity

Friction is a force that occurs when two surfaces come in contact, such as when a book is pushed across a desk. Friction creates a gripping action that affects how much work is needed to move an object. When friction is greater, more work is needed. For pulleys, the contact between the rope and the wheel creates friction. The amount of force needed to overcome this friction is usually low. This makes the pulley an **efficient** machine for doing work.

Another force affecting how much work is needed to move an object is **gravity**. Earth's gravity pulls down on objects. This makes them harder to move.

Mass vs. Weight

Mass is how much material an object contains. Weight is how strongly gravity pulls on an object. An object's mass affects its weight. A rock has more mass than a marshmallow the same size, so the rock weighs more on Earth. However, mass and weight are not the same.

Mass is often measured in kilograms (kg). A person with a mass of 91 kilograms weighs 200 pounds on Earth. This is because Earth's gravity pulls on a 91-kilogram mass with a force of 200 pounds. The Moon has much weaker gravity, so the same person weighs less there. The Moon's gravity pulls on a 91-kilogram mass with a force of only 33 pounds. That same person has almost no weight on a spacecraft because there is little gravity. He or she weighs about 0 pounds, even though the person's mass is still 91 kilograms.

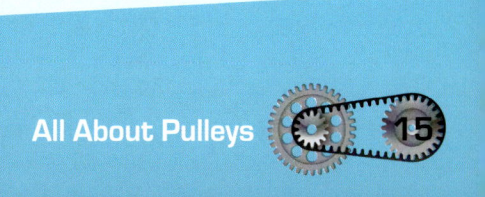

All About Pulleys

Working with Force

In science, work happens when a force is used to move an object over a distance. For work to happen, the force must be applied in the same direction the object is moving. Lifting a rock off the ground is work because the force applied to pull the rock up is going in the same upward direction that the rock is moving.

Work also happens when a person pushes a rock forward along the ground. However, pushing against a very heavy rock and failing to move it is not work. The person may feel tired from his or her effort. Yet, if the rock has not moved, no work has taken place.

Tugboats do work when they use pulleys to pull much larger boats.

As the force needed to move an object increases, the work involved in moving it also increases. This also applies to distance. The amount of work needed to move the object increases as the distance the object must move increases.

Simple machines make doing work easier. They do this by changing the amount and the direction of the force needed to move an object. Although less force is needed, simple machines require moving a greater distance.

Calculating Work

The amount of work needed to lift a 10-pound (4.5-kg) ball changes based on the distance it is lifted. To calculate the work, the weight of the ball is multiplied by the height it will be moved.

10 x 2 = 20

It takes 20 pounds (9.1 kg) of effort to lift the ball 2 feet (0.6 m).

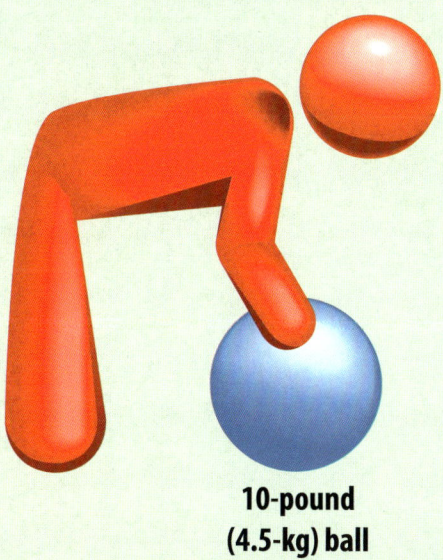

10-pound (4.5-kg) ball

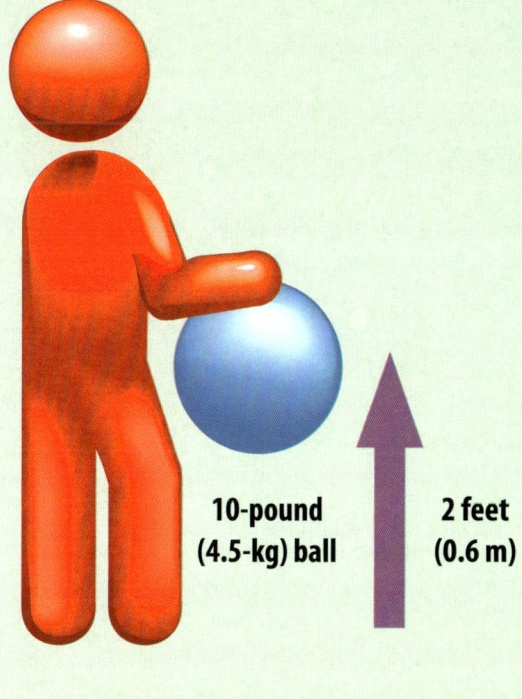

10-pound (4.5-kg) ball

2 feet (0.6 m)

All About Pulleys

A single movable pulley is free to move up and down.

How Pulleys Work

Some types of pulleys make work easier because they offer a **mechanical advantage**. This means these pulleys require less force to move an object than would be needed without the pulley. One of the simplest kinds of pulley is the single movable pulley. Using this type of pulley requires only half the force that would be needed to lift a load straight up.

When a person pulls on a rope attached to a single movable pulley, the force needed to move the load is spread over the rope on both sides of the pulley. It is as if the rope were being pulled from both sides at once. The change in the force needed to move the load comes with an increase in the distance the person must move. A single movable pulley needs less force but more distance to move a load.

Calculating Effort

The amount of effort needed to lift a 10-pound (4.5-kg) load changes based on the type of pulley being used. The pulley on the left is a fixed pulley, which means the pulley does not move and the same amount of effort is needed to lift the load. The pulley on the right is a movable pulley, which reduces the effort needed to lift the load by half.

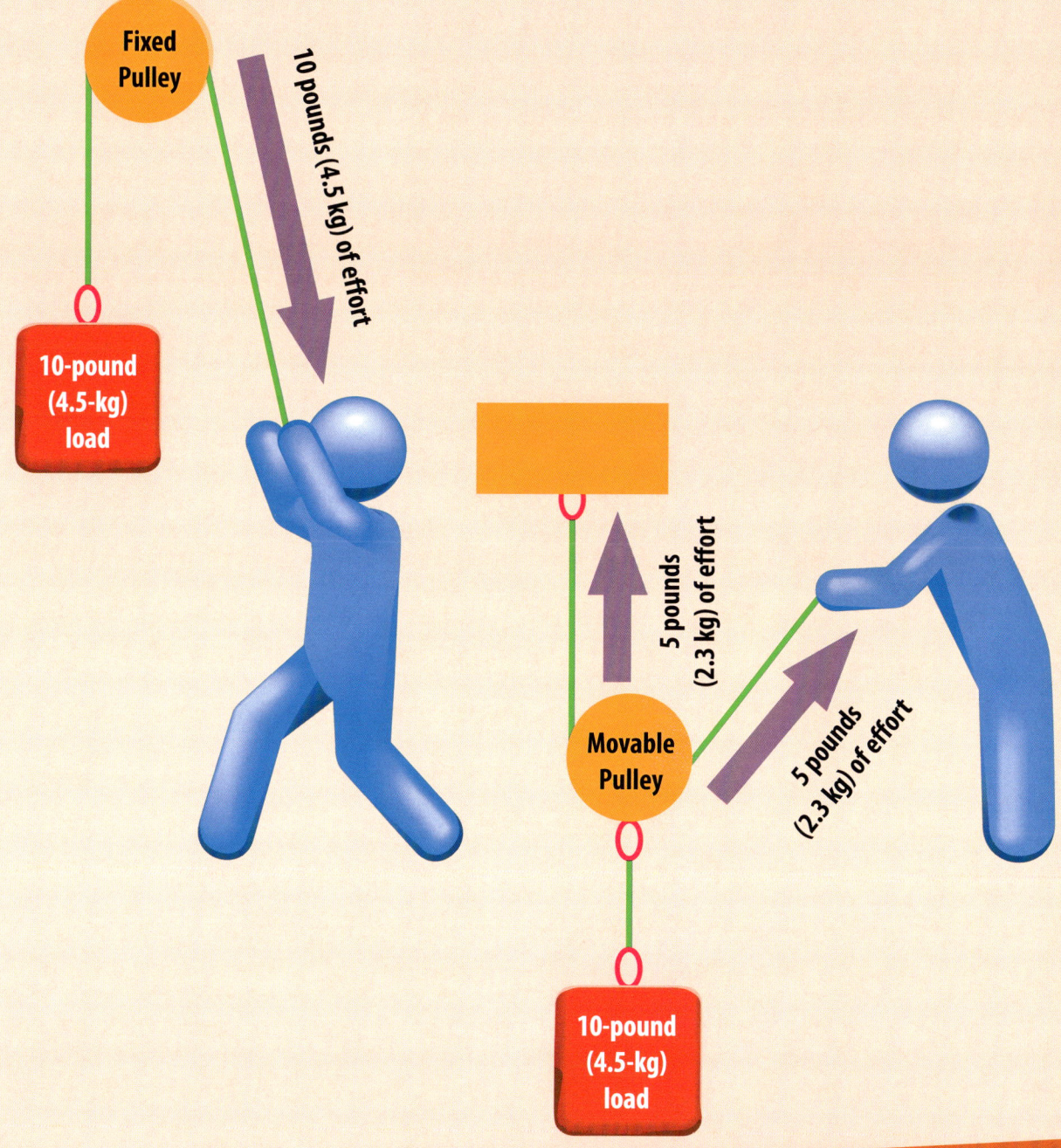

What Is a Manufacturing Engineer?

Manufacturing **engineers** help design and build factories. They may use their understanding of simple machines, such as pulleys, to make factories work more safely. Manufacturing engineers often help **automate** factories, so that robots instead of people can perform dangerous tasks or work that does not require skills. Manufacturing engineers must go to school for many years to gain the knowledge needed to succeed in their job.

Henry Ford

Henry Ford, born in 1863 in Michigan, was an engineer and businessman. He founded the Ford Motor Company in 1903. Ford introduced the assembly line in his factory. It allowed workers to stay in one spot while the car being built came to them on a conveyor belt. Workers were able to produce one automobile, called the Model T, every 24 seconds. Ford's assembly line reduced the cost of making cars, so that millions of people could afford to buy one.

Manufacturing engineers often visit the factory floor.

Simple Machines

Brain Teasers

1 What are the six simple machines?

2 What is a winch?

3 Which type of pulley operates with a belt?

4 What is a fixed pulley?

5 Who invented the compound pulley in about 250 BC?

6 In what year was Notre Dame Cathedral in Paris completed?

7 Who invented the tow truck in 1916?

8 What is friction?

9 What kind of engineer helps design and build factories?

10 Who founded the Ford Motor Company in 1903?

ANSWERS: 1. The six simple machines are the inclined plane, the lever, the pulley, the screw, the wedge, and the wheel and axle. 2. A winch is a drum with cables wound around it. 3. A belt drive or a drive belt operates with a belt instead of a rope or cable. 4. A fixed pulley is held in place at a single spot. 5. The ancient Greek scientist Archimedes invented the compound pulley in about 250 BC. 6. Notre Dame Cathedral in Paris was completed in 1345. 7. Ernest Holmes invented the tow truck, which uses pulleys to lift cars, in 1916. 8. Friction is a force that occurs when two surfaces come in contact. 9. Manufacturing engineers help design and build factories. 10. Henry Ford founded the Ford Motor Company in 1903.

All About Pulleys 21

Pulleys in Action

Make a pulley to lift objects more easily.

Materials Needed

long string

bottle of water

door and doorknob handle

Directions

1 Tie one end of the string to the spout of the water bottle.

2 Place the string in the groove, or middle part, of the doorknob between the doorknob and the door. Make sure that the bottle is on one side of the grooved area of the doorknob. The other side of the string should be on the opposite side of the doorknob.

3 Pull the free end of the string downward. As you pull the string down, the bottle will move higher. Is there any friction slowing down the string as you pull it?

Simple Machines

Key Words

automate: to make the way something works, such as a machine, automatic

axle: a shaft on which one or more wheels turn

cable: a rope-like device made of metal wires that are twisted together

conveyor belt: a moving belt that operates over pulleys to transport materials

efficient: producing a desired result from as little effort as possible

effort: the power being used to move an object

energy: the power needed to do work

engineers: people who use science to solve practical problems

gear: a wheel with teeth on its edge

gravity: a force that pulls objects toward one another

mechanical advantage: a measure of how much easier a task is made when a simple machine is used

rudder: a movable piece of an aircraft's tail used for steering

work: power applied over distance to move an object

Index

Archimedes 12, 13

belt drive 8

Colosseum 12, 13
compound pulley 9, 12, 13
conveyor belt 13, 20

effort 4, 9, 16, 17, 19
elevator 4
equilibrium 14

fixed pulley 9, 19
force 14, 15, 16, 17, 18
Ford, Henry 13, 20
friction 15, 22

gravity 15

Holmes, Ernest 13

inclined plane 4, 6

Leonardo da Vinci 4
lever 4, 6, 7
load 4, 6, 7, 8, 9, 18, 19

manufacturing engineer 20
mass 15
mechanical advantage 18
Mirabella V 13
Mount Everest 11
movable pulley 9, 18, 19

Notre Dame Cathedral 12, 13

polar bears 10

rollercoaster 13

sailboats 9, 13
screw 4, 6, 7

wedge 4, 6, 7
weight 8, 14, 15, 17
wheel and axle 4, 6, 7
work 4, 15, 16, 17, 18

zip line 10

All About Pulleys

+ SUPPLEMENTARY RESOURCES

Click on the plus icon ✚ found in the bottom left corner of each spread to open additional teacher resources.

- Download and print the book's quizzes and activities
- Access curriculum correlations
- Explore additional web applications that enhance the Lightbox experience

LIGHTBOX DIGITAL TITLES
Packed full of integrated media

VIDEOS

INTERACTIVE MAPS

WEBLINKS

SLIDESHOWS

QUIZZES

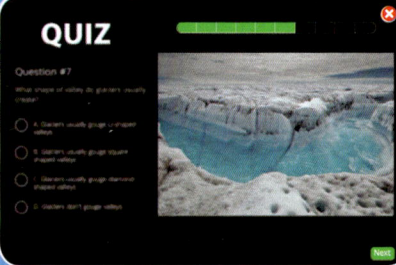

OPTIMIZED FOR
✓ **TABLETS**
✓ **WHITEBOARDS**
✓ **COMPUTERS**
✓ **AND MUCH MORE!**

Published by Smartbook Media Inc.
350 5th Avenue, 59th Floor
New York, NY 10118
Website: www.openlightbox.com

Copyright © 2017 Smartbook Media Inc.
All rights reserved. No part of this publication may be reproduced, stored in a retrieval system, or transmitted in any form or by any means, electronic, mechanical, photocopying, recording, or otherwise, without the prior written permission of the publisher.

Library of Congress Control Number:
2016935458

ISBN 978-1-5105-0954-2 (hardcover)
ISBN 978-1-5105-0956-6 (multi-user eBook)

Printed in Brainerd, Minnesota, United States
1 2 3 4 5 6 7 8 9 0   20 19 18 17 16

032016
090316

Project Coordinator Heather Kissock
Art Director Terry Paulhus

Photo Credits
Every reasonable effort has been made to trace ownership and to obtain permission to reprint copyright material. The publisher would be pleased to have any errors or omissions brought to its attention so that they may be corrected in subsequent printings. The publisher acknowledges Getty Images, Corbis, and iStock as its primary image suppliers for this title.